To my family for their unconditional love and unfaltering support,
I love you.

To everyone who has supported me through times of challenge and difficulty,
I thank you from the bottom of my heart.

- Louise -

NOTE TO THE READER

The first time that I'd heard of OCD (Obsessive Compulsive Disorder) was at the age of 14 when I received my diagnosis. I had no idea what it was but there was some relief in knowing that there was a name for what was going on inside my head and that I wasn't alone, as it is more common than I'd realised.

Before being diagnosed, I felt trapped inside my mind and alone in my thoughts and had no idea how to escape the overwhelming thoughts I was experiencing. I would worry constantly and the only way I could make it better was to carry out rituals which I believed was overpowering the thought. Without realising, I was actually feeding the anxiety and the thoughts would soon return bigger, stronger and more frequently. I got to a point where I could not manage my anxiety alone and I was referred to a child psychologist to help me to understand what was going on inside my mind and help me take back control of my thoughts in a way that suited me. Over the years I have tried different therapy options including CBT (Cognitive Behavioural Therapy) to gradually expose myself to my fears, in the hope to one day overcome some of them and it has provided me with stepping stones to get to where I am today.

Growing up, I was very different from those around me and I quickly became aware of the lack of understanding and misconceptions of OCD and its impact on not only the sufferer but those around them too. I now work as an ELSA (Emotional Literacy Support Assistant) within a primary school setting, helping children and giving them a safe space to talk through any worries or concerns and helping them to find strategies to help manage their anxiety effectively.

The idea behind this book is to raise awareness and to give an insight into OCD and the impact it has on a person's life, whilst trying to positively highlight that with the right support, it can be managed effectively. Choosing to seek professional help, along with the love and support of my family, teachers and others around me, helped me to build on my confidence and achieve things I never thought possible. Throughout this book I have used my professional knowledge, alongside my personal experience of OCD, to create a story that will be beneficial to both children and adults and help them to understand the complexity of OCD and how it can be managed with the right support and guidance.

- Louise Buckner -

Phoebe was fearful, she feared many things, big things, small things and almost everything in-between. She was always worrying and checking things, everything had to be clean and 'right' before she could continue with her day.

Every morning, Phoebe would check things like if the lights were off, if her bag was packed ready for school, if her pens were lined up correctly, if the hamster cage was closed, if the taps were off, that her family were safe and that the door was shut… all this before going to school. Phoebe was always thinking about her fears and how she could put them right. Just a little tap, counting to a certain number or a safety word would have the power to cancel out the thought, was what Phoebe truly believed.

In the car, on the way to school, Phoebe's mind would wander. The thoughts would reappear and she would replay her actions in her head – just to stop the doubting voices she could hear in her head.

'Was the hamster cage closed?'

Yes, I remember checking it.

'Were the taps turned off?'

Yes, I'm sure I checked.

Doubting herself was something Phoebe often did and she started rummaging through her bag as the car pulled into the school grounds.

'Phoebe you're going to be late for the register,' warned her Mum.

'If you hadn't spent so long in the bathroom this morning then we'd have been here ages ago,' her Mum said crossly.

Phoebe hated being late for school and this only added to her fears as she anxiously stepped out of the car.

Arriving at her desk, Phoebe began her daily routine of unpacking her things, organising them neatly in a row along the top of her table but most importantly, checking that her desk was clean.

'Phoebe, we have this conversation every morning, please stop fiddling it is awfully distracting,' declared her teacher, Miss Huggleton.

No matter how much Phoebe feared getting into trouble and no matter how hard she tried, she just could not dismiss the thoughts telling her to straighten the ruler or move the rubber 1cm to the right but this only acted as a magnet to the class as suddenly all eyes were on Phoebe.

'Phoebe Neville,' bellowed Miss Huggleton, 'I will not ask you again.'

Phoebe felt her face turn as red as a tomato, as sniggers echoed around the classroom. She felt so embarrassed. Phoebe knew that her behaviour was not 'normal' but at the same time she just had to respond to the thoughts in her head.

Throughout the day Phoebe would check things, ask questions, check again, do things to make her fears go away, before worrying about the next thing. All this seemed strange and somewhat funny to her class friends who would point and laugh at her.

'Why can't they see that if I don't check and put things right, then something terrible is going to happen and it will be all my fault' wondered Phoebe.

Arriving home that afternoon, Phoebe rushed upstairs to get changed and wash her hands before dinner, pretty normal right? Well not for Phoebe, she would have to do things in the correct order, count to 100 or until her hands felt clean enough. She did this as she thought it was the only way to make sure she didn't make her house dirty or make her family ill. Phoebe was tired but still she had to make sure she listened to her thoughts.

'What are you doing in there?' questioned Phoebe's Mum.

'I will be there in a minute,' snapped Phoebe.

‘This is the fourth time I’ve called you and dinner is getting cold,’ insisted her Mum.

‘I know it’s the fourth time because every time you interrupt me, I have to start all over again’ thought a frustrated Phoebe.

During dinner, sensing her Mum and Dad's frustration, Phoebe couldn't keep it to herself any longer and decided it was time to tell them just how troublesome her thoughts had become. She was sad, confused, frustrated, felt guilty and told her parents how she wished she could be normal like the other kids in her class.

That night as Phoebe listened from the top of the staircase, she heard her parents discussing her recent change in behaviour. She could hear the sadness in their voices and through muffled speech she heard her Mum say that her teacher, Miss Huggleton was concerned too and that it was time to see Doctor Charlston.

'Doctor Charlston is the doctor that Daddy saw when he got really sad at work and that Mrs Schwarz from the corner shop saw when she started to worry about things' Phoebe thought curiously.

The following week, whilst sat in Doctor Charlston's waiting room, Phoebe's fears were HUGE. Why was she there? Was she in trouble? What was Doctor Charlston going to say?

Suddenly, her thoughts were interrupted by a friendly voice calling her name.

Phoebe stepped cautiously into Doctor Charlston's office and he greeted her with a warm, friendly smile before guiding her over to the comfy chair directly opposite to his.

'Hello Phoebe, I'm Doctor Charlston. Now, I hear you have been having a bit of a tricky time recently and have been trying your best to manage things by yourself but your parents feel that now you could do with a bit of help. Would you like to tell me all about it?'

Doctor Charlston was a big man, with broad shoulders, a big bushy beard but a very kind face. He was very friendly and made Phoebe feel relaxed and he seemed to know all the right things to say.

As Phoebe started to talk to Doctor Charlston, she felt as if all those things that she had been keeping to herself suddenly felt a little bit lighter. Somehow, sharing her thoughts with someone else felt like a big relief.

Phoebe told him about her fears, starting with the small things all the way up to the big things. She told him that she felt guilty for her behaviour and how it affected her parents, teachers and her friendships.

Doctor Charlston listened carefully, gave reassuring nods in the right places and only when Phoebe felt she had said everything, did he begin to explain things to Phoebe and her parents.

PHOEBE

Phoebe's behaviour was something that Doctor Charlston had seen before. Over the years he had seen many people, young and old, with similar worries. He explained that Phoebe was suffering from something called Obsessive Compulsive Disorder or OCD for short and that it was more common than people realise.

Suddenly Phoebe didn't feel so alone with her thoughts and it felt as if someone had just lifted a heavy rucksack from her back.

'OCD is when your fear becomes so powerful and it causes you to be anxious or scared. It isn't nice to feel anxious or afraid but fear is our brain's way of letting us know when we're in danger,' Doctor Charlston explained.

‘It tells us to be alert and respond to those dangers and although a healthy level of fear is necessary to keep us safe, the anxiety that comes with OCD is different as it can cause scary, upsetting thoughts that lead you into carrying out unusual behaviours or key phrases to overpower the danger.’

‘These behaviours are called rituals, which you do to help make your worries feel a little better, until they return again,’ he continued.

Phoebe nodded as she felt the tears roll down her face. Doctor Charlston was describing exactly how she felt.

'You see, fears and worries are OK to have in small amounts, we all get them, even me, sometimes these fears can grow and become too much for us to manage on our own.'

'Everyone's mind works differently but by sharing our thoughts with a trusted adult, it can help us find ways to manage them together,' advised Doctor Charlston.

That night Phoebe thought about everything that Doctor Charlston had said, she felt confident that having someone to share her concerns with would be helpful.

Mum was going to arrange with the school for Phoebe to see Mrs Shenton, the lady who helps children with their worries and concerns, who would give her a safe space at school to discuss any worries she may have and Doctor Charlston was going to arrange for Phoebe to see a lady called Doctor Spellman who specialised in helping children with OCD.

Over the following weeks Phoebe found comfort in talking things through with Mrs Shenton at school and having fortnightly sessions with Doctor Spellman.

Doctor Spellman was a kind lady who helped Phoebe to understand what was going on in her mind. She explained that Phoebe's OCD meant that she would focus on a worry so much, that it wouldn't go away and this would cause all the scary thoughts, images and urges to get stuck in her mind.

This would mean that Phoebe would try to do rituals like doing or saying certain things to make herself feel safe.

‘Fears are like seeds, the more you water them, the bigger they grow. Your fears have now become phobias and by doing the rituals or avoiding certain situations, you are feeding your worry and making it bigger,’ Doctor Spellman told Phoebe.

As time went on, Phoebe had good weeks and bad weeks, some days her worries were less and other days more but she worked hard to cut back on her rituals a little at a time. Although it would be a long road and sometimes very tough Phoebe never gave up and would remember the first piece of advice that Doctor Spellman told her...

'You can't get to the top of the ladder without climbing each step first.'

Phoebe knew that with the help and support of her family, teachers and Doctor Spellman that she could start to manage her fears in her own time and in a way that worked for her.

Phoebe learnt to accept her OCD and little by little she started to build confidence and take back control of her mind. She realised that although she still had fears and 'what if' moments, that if she used her new coping strategies, she could manage them successfully and most importantly to Phoebe, she could be just like all the other kids in class.

ABOUT THE AUTHOR

Louise Buckner was born and raised in a small town in Berkshire, England. A former Healthcare Assistant, Louise now works in a primary school in Berkshire as a fully trained Emotional Literacy Support Assistant, helping children to understand their feelings and emotions by teaching them coping strategies to manage them effectively. Louise also teaches Spanish as a Modern Foreign Language and finds delight in watching the children enjoy learning new skills.

In her spare time, Louise has spent time studying various areas of mental health and wellbeing and has gained a diploma in Child Psychology Level 4, which she passed with a distinction, as well as gaining a qualification in Child and Adolescent Counselling.

Louise is very family orientated and enjoys spending time with them and creating memories. She enjoys spending her spare time reading, listening to music, writing short stories and poetry as well as going to the theatre.

Diagnosed with chronic OCD at the age of 14 and the journey that followed, along with her passion for helping others, has been the inspiration behind writing this book. Louise hopes to address misconceptions of OCD and send out a message that it is OK to need and ask for help in order to manage anxiety effectively.

First published in paperback by
Michael Terence Publishing in 2020
www.mtp.agency

ISBN 9781913653705

Illustrations
by Tom Burchell

Printed in Poland
by Amazon Fulfillment
Poland Sp. z o.o., Wrocław

62096014R00026